By Chance?

LANDSCAPES FROM THE CANVAS OF THE CREATOR

JOHN MACMURRAY

MULTNOMAH PUBLISHERS · SISTERS, OREGON

I owe a debt of gratitude to a host of people who have encouraged and assisted me in making my vision a reality. I especially want to thank my dad, my sister Judy, and her husband, Girard, who have always supported me in every way; my mom and my brother Charlie, who have passed away and met the Creator; my wife, Terri, and children, Chris and Elle, for their unwavering love; and the good friends at Calvary Fellowship Church, who gave me my first camera. Little did they know...

I also thank the Creator, who not only made nature beautiful, but also made us with the ability to appreciate it.

John MacMurray
c/o Multnomah Publishers
Post Office Box 1720
Sisters, Oregon 97759

BY CHANCE?
published by Multnomah Publishers, Inc.

© 1998 by John MacMurray
International Standard Book Number: 1-57673-297-5

Design by D² DesignWorks

Scripture quotations are from:
The Holy Bible, New International Version
© 1973, 1978, 1984 by the International Bible Society
used by permission of Zondervan Bible Publishers

Printed in China

For information:
MULTNOMAH PUBLISHERS, INC.
POST OFFICE BOX 1720
SISTERS, OREGON 97759

98 99 00 01 02 03 04 — 10 9 8 7 6 5 4 3 2

To all those who seek the
Designer of the grand design

This a piece too fair

To be the child of Chance,

and not of Care.

No Atoms casually together hurl'd

Could e'er produce so beautiful a world.

JOHN DRYDEN

There is nothing unusual about the drive on Highway 180 north from Flagstaff, Arizona. The scenery is unremarkable: flat terrain with the occasional desert pine or juniper tree dotting the landscape. But for me,

a young man of twenty-six visiting the area for the first time, the ride was filled with excitement and anticipation. Within the hour, I was to behold one of the greatest natural wonders of the United States of America.

It was a bright, cloudless day, and the sun was warm on my face. My excitement grew as I approached the entrance. But to my dismay, the only change in scenery as I entered the park was that the trees grew denser. Disappointment crept over me, dampening my enthusiasm for what I had thought of as the highlight of my cross-country adventure. Where was the great wonder I had heard so much about?

I came to the first turnout and immediately pulled my car into the parking lot. The sign read *Mather Point,* but I still couldn't see anything. As I began following the walkway, I became anxious and a little perplexed. Why couldn't I see something so enormous when I was so close?

Suddenly I broke through some trees, and there it was. A vista so stupendous, so fantastic, it seemed to explode in front of my eyes. *Grand* seems almost trite when used to describe such a place. It borders on incomprehensible. But Incomprehensible Canyon doesn't have quite the same ring, does it? The word *awesome,* in its traditional sense, is a word that is truly appropriate for the Grand Canyon.

For the next few hours I gazed, my eyes absorbing a view so marvelous that I was filled with wonder. As the sun crept closer to the horizon, light danced on the rocks, changing colors, creating shadows and depth. With each passing minute, the canyon became more breathtaking. It was one of those moments you savor in life. Faced with a beauty and majesty that dwarfed me, I felt small, and at the same time, utterly satisfied.

Rather abruptly, a man who was standing near me spoke. Since no one else was within fifty feet of us, I assumed he spoke to me. I will never forget his words: "Isn't it amazing what evolution has done?"

"I was thinking the very opposite of that," I replied. "I'm amazed at what God has created."

He chuckled as if to say, "I can't believe that you believe that outdated idea!" In fact, as we continued our conversation, he explicitly stated that attitude.

When the sky grew dark, signaling the end of the show, we both went our separate ways. Although I never knew his name, our encounter had a profound effect on my life. Two people, same place, same view, but two world views. What had been a brief conversation between strangers lingered in my mind, eventually becoming the impetus for this book.

This experience also brought something more important into view. I began to realize that there is a question that arises in anyone who is confronted with the majestic beauty of nature. The question comes in various forms, but essentially is this: who or what is responsible for nature's existence? How we answer this directly affects our perception of nature itself.

Two views compete for our attention and loyalty: Some attribute nature's order, complexity, and beauty to coincidence. Others perceive nature as the work of a personal Creator.

It was on the rim of the Grand Canyon that I answered this question for myself. The sense of awe and wonder that I experienced came not only from the beauty of the scene, but also from the seemingly incomprehensible idea that there exists a being who designed it. I began to realize that my view and appreciation of nature was undeniably linked to my view of the existence of a personal Creator. Like a painting and its painter or a poem and its poet, the creation displays the brilliance of the Creator.

How often have we heard the natural world referred to as "Mother Nature"? Often we personify nature, giving it a godlike status. But if nature is the result of chance, then why would we seek to personalize the impersonal? Could it be that nature itself leads us to believe that it was designed? This overwhelming sense of design is precisely the reason so many conclude there exists a Creator behind the creation.

The natural world is a wonderful and beautiful thing to behold. Most people, even casual observers, recognize the orderliness, complexity, and sheer majesty of the beauty found in nature. Our emotional responses to nature—fulfillment, satisfaction, awe—are experiences we all enjoy.

Imagine a clear evening: the sun slips below the horizon, and its last rays fire wisps of clouds with colors of red, gold, and orange. Is there anyone who would perceive this scene as ugly? Oh, many might not be interested or would prefer something different, but no one would find the sunset distasteful. Universally, not only do we agree on what is beautiful, but we also possess the ability to recognize beauty. Could the definition and recognition of beauty in our world develop universally by chance? Or was the natural world designed and we along with it so that we could recognize and enjoy the beauty around us? Likewise, we all recognize order in our world, but how did it become orderly, and how did we acquire the ability to recognize this order? Even assuming that order was created out of chaos, it would be incredible to think that we have acquired the ability to perceive order from something that was, in itself, not ordered.

The problem that we all face in seeking an answer to nature's origin, regardless of what view we hold, is that no one witnessed the beginning of nature's existence. Both the creation and coincidence views are belief systems. What each of us must do is to choose the view that makes the most sense with the information we possess.

As I journey through nature's landscapes, my wonder is renewed at the beauty I continue to discover. Color, light, and form are joined in a never-ending dance, weaving a tapestry of beauty in our world. This collection of images is part of my ongoing attempt to capture the miracle of nature's beauty. Think of each of the photographs as a small window providing a brief glimpse of the Creator. My hope is that these images will evoke in you a sense of awe similar to what I experienced at the Grand Canyon. Drink in the forms, light, and color that blend to construct the beauty you see in the photographs. And ask yourself, did all this happen by chance?

JOHN MACMURRAY

FORM

We ponder it. We marvel at it. It may be the symmetry of a snow-capped peak rising out of lush green forest or the serene, serpentine path of a river; the otherworldly experience of hiking past the peculiar shapes of arches, spires, and buttes in canyons and plateaus; or just gazing at clouds and imagining the familiar. Form fascinates us and amazes us. Without form, light and color would not have a stage.

Form throughout the natural world is characterized by two words: uniformity and diversity. General forms, such as waves, mountain peaks, or trees, exhibit uniformity. Even the physical laws, which govern the shaping of our world, function in an orderly and dependable manner. This uniformity suggests order, yet within this uniformity, there is an incredible diversity. How many different trees or flowers exist in the world? A botanist would be hard-pressed to name them all. This diversity suggests creativity.

If order and creativity coexist in our natural world in a dependable fashion, then it is strongly implied that there exists design. And design demands a designer.

The more I study nature, the more I stand amazed at the work of the Creator.

LOUIS PASTEUR

GRAND TETON NATIONAL PARK, WYOMING

The contemplation

of a beautiful landscape excites the highest

spiritual pleasure in us.

Death Valley National Monument, California

Elowah Falls, Columbia River Gorge, Oregon

MONO LAKE, CALIFORNIA

WILDFLOWERS, MOUNT RAINIER, WASHINGTON

TURRET ARCH, ARCHES NATIONAL PARK, UTAH

WILDCAT CREEK BASIN, CANADA

There is something in the depths of our souls
which tells us that the world may be more than a
mere combination of events.

LOUIS PASTEUR

SLOT CANYON, ARIZONA

HARRIMAN FIORD, ALASKA

It is the sheer universality of perfection,

the fact that everywhere we look, to whatever depth we look,

we find an elegance and ingenuity of an absolute transcending quality,

which so mitigates against the idea of chance.

MICHAEL DENTON

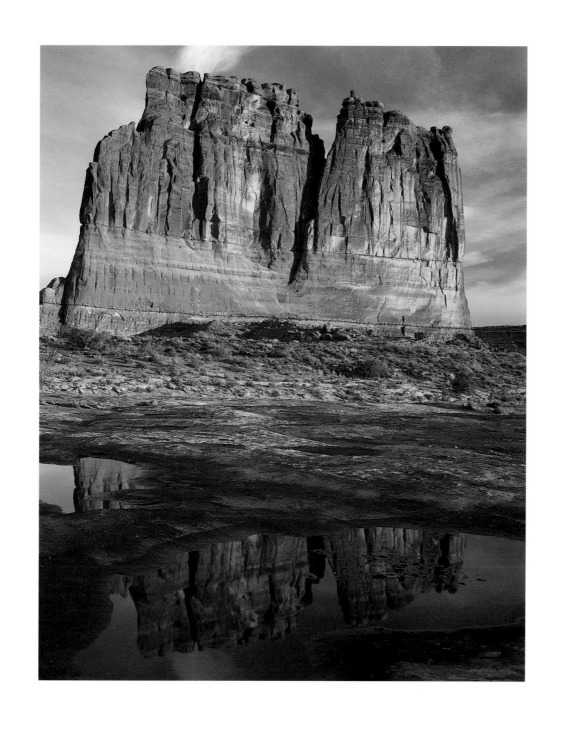

OCEANSIDE, OREGON

COURTHOUSE TOWER, ARCHES NATIONAL PARK, UTAH

23

ARCHES NATIONAL PARK, UTAH

THE GATEWAY, ALASKA RANGE, ALASKA

For since the creation of the world God's invisible qualities—

his eternal power and divine nature—have been clearly seen,

being understood from what has been made.

UPPER HORSETAIL FALLS, COLUMBIA RIVER GORGE, OREGON

KALALAU VALLEY, KAUAI, HAWAII

26

The significance and joy in my science comes in those

occasional moments of discovering something new and saying to myself,

"So that's how God did it."

HENRY F. SCHAEFER

CIRQUE OF THE TOWERS, WIND RIVER WILDERNESS, WYOMING

Deadhorse Point, Canyonlands National Park, Utah

EL CAPITAN, GUADALUPE NATIONAL PARK, TEXAS

MERCED RIVER, YOSEMITE NATIONAL PARK, CALIFORNIA

Yet this glorious valley might well be called a church,

for every lover of the great Creator who comes within the broad overwhelming

influences of the place fails not to worship as they never did before.

JOHN MUIR

In particular the great Valley has always kept a place in my mind.

How did the Lord make it? What tools did He use?

How did He apply them and when?

JOHN MUIR ON THE YOSEMITE VALLEY

LIGHT

Natural light is a wonder. It fires the sky at sunset. It sparkles off the new-fallen snow as though diamonds were scattered across the earth. It warms the forests and meadows with a golden glow. It dances on the waters of mountain lakes and streams.

Natural light creates an emotional response in us: The exhilaration of a bright, cloudless morning. The awe of the power of jagged lightning. The peacefulness of light filtering through a fog-shrouded forest.

Natural light brings diversity to the landscape. The shadows and colors it creates can change the landscape even as you watch. Light is the evidence that, on the landscape, creativity is not just a thing of the past, but is the present, ongoing reality of natural beauty.

How wholly infused with God is this one big word of love that we call the world!

JOHN MUIR

LORD FLAT, HELLS CANYON, OREGON

Do you not know? Have you not heard?

The Lord is the everlasting God, the Creator of

the ends of the earth.

ISAIAH 40:28

GLEN COE, SCOTLAND

TOROWEEP POINT, GRAND CANYON NATIONAL PARK, ARIZONA

The orderliness of the universe is the supreme discovery in science.

F. R. MOULTON

CHADDS FORD, PENNSYLVANIA

UPPER REDFISH LAKE, SAWTOOTH WILDERNESS, IDAHO

ST. MARY LAKE, MONTANA

RAIN FOREST, ECOLA STATE PARK, OREGON

I believe in Christianity as I believe

that the sun has risen. Not only because I see it,

but because I see everything by it.

C. S. LEWIS

ST. MARY LAKE, MONTANA

MILFORD SOUND, FIORDLAND NATIONAL PARK, NEW ZEALAND

It is difficult, when looking at such extravagant inventiveness,

to avoid the question: why is so much of nature so unnecessarily beautiful?

GORDON STAINFORTH

NAPALI COASTLINE, KAUAI, HAWAII

MOUNT ST. HELENS NATIONAL VOLCANIC MONUMENT, WASHINGTON

McGowan Peak, Sawtooth Wilderness, Idaho

Prince William Sound, Alaska

Apart from the idea of design and purpose

it seems impossible to understand this universe of which we are a part.

WARREN C. YOUNG

The mountains have all the appearance of being

the work of a creative imagination.

GORDON STAINFORTH

MOUNT HOOD AND LOST LAKE, OREGON

GLEN SHIEL, SCOTLAND

THE NEEDLES, CANNON BEACH, OREGON

SCOTT CREEK BEACH, OLYMPIC NATIONAL PARK, WASHINGTON

By faith we understand that the universe

was formed at God's command, so that what is seen was

not made out of what was visible.

HEBREWS 11:3

JOHN DAY FOSSIL BEDS, PAINTED HILLS UNIT, OREGON

RAIN FOREST, BRAULIO CARRILLO NATIONAL PARK, COSTA RICA

There is something which is directing the universe,

and which appears to me as a law.... I think we have to assume it is more like a mind...

you can hardly imagine a bit of matter giving instructions.

COLOR

People often ask me, "Where is your favorite place to photograph?" I usually respond that I don't have one favorite place. But I do have favorite kinds of photographs. Among these are photographs that reflect the vibrant color in nature.

Color in our natural world is a purely aesthetic quality for us. We all find enjoyment and pleasure in the color we see in nature, from the deep green of the primeval forest to the sparkling turquoise of the tropical ocean to the intense red of sandstone in the last light of day. Who has not enjoyed the rainbow of colors found in the sunset or a carpet of wildflowers in a mountain meadow?

Color contributes greatly to our perception of beauty and diversity in nature. From muted pastels to rich, saturated hues, color abounds in the natural world. Drink in its beauty. Revel in its diversity.

With regard to the origin of life, science... positively affirms creative power.

LORD KELVIN

GLACIER NATIONAL PARK, MONTANA

LATOURELL FALLS, COLUMBIA RIVER GORGE, OREGON

STRAWBERRY HEDGEHOG CACTUS, HARCUVAR MOUNTAINS, ARIZONA

I am filled with wonder as I look at nature,

to see how God technically did it and realized the beauty

of His own soul in doing it.

MOUNT HOOD, OREGON

LOWER PROXY FALLS, THREE SISTERS WILDERNESS, OREGON

We know perfectly well that if you leave matter to itself,

it does not organize itself—in spite of all the efforts in recent years to prove that it does.

ARTHUR E. WILDER-SMITH

SPARKS LAKE, SOUTH SISTER MOUNTAIN, OREGON

ECOLA STATE PARK, OREGON

63

Paradise Meadow, Mount Rainier National Park, Washington

Park Avenue, Arches National Park, Utah

MOUNT MCKINLEY, DENALI NATIONAL PARK, ALASKA

WASATCH NATIONAL FOREST, UTAH

I shall never believe that God plays dice with the world.

ALBERT EINSTEIN

THE TWELVE APOSTLES, AUSTRALIA

BRACKEN IN FOREST, SCOTLAND

When I look at the solar system,

I see the earth at the right distance from the sun to receive the proper

amounts of heat and light. This did not happen by chance.

Sneffels Range, Uncompahgre National Forest, Colorado

Monkey Flowers, Mount Jefferson Wilderness, Oregon

71

Big Sur Coastline, California

Hells Canyon, Oregon

No philosophical theory which I have yet

come across is a radical improvement on the words of Genesis,

that "In the beginning God made heaven and earth."

C. S. LEWIS

FALLEN LEAVES, GROTON STATE FOREST, VERMONT

CARP RIVER, PORCUPINE MOUNTAIN STATE PARK, MICHIGAN

MANUEL ANTONIO NATIONAL PARK, COSTA RICA

WILDFLOWER MEADOW, DOG MOUNTAIN, COLUMBIA RIVER GORGE, WASHINGTON

The two alternatives are very clear cut.

Either there is a personal beginning to everything or one has what the impersonal

throws up by chance out of the time sequence.

FRANCIS A. SCHAEFFER